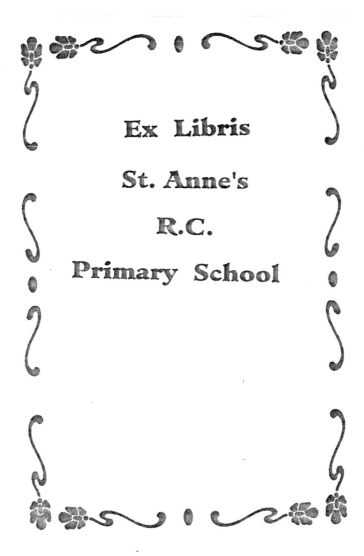

Ex Libris

St. Anne's

R.C.

Primary School

BREAD UPON THE WATERS

Derek Worlock

Archbishop of Liverpool

Bread
upon the Waters

The living faith of Liverpool

 St Paul Publications

St Paul Publications
Middlegreen, Slough SL3 6BT, United Kingdom

© St Paul Publications UK 1991
Cover design by Diane Edwards
Cover photo © Merseyside Tourism Board
Photos by Tom Murphy
ISBN 085439 394 3
Printed by Biddles Ltd, Guildford

St Paul Publications is an activity of the priests and brothers of
the Society of St Paul who proclaim the Gospel through the
media of social communication

Contents

Introduction

On the feast of Pentecost in 1981 Pope John Paul II celebrated Mass in the Metropolitan Cathedral in Liverpool. Afterwards he went out to the piazza behind the Cathedral, where he was received with great enthusiasm by several thousand young people who were waiting there to greet him. Mostly clad in the red T-shirts of the Youth Service, they cheered, they prayed and they sang hymns and songs for him. Then they linked arms and broke into their favourite anthem, 'Bind us together, Lord', followed with rather greater abandon by 'In my Liverpool home'.

The Pope watched and applauded them. Then with great deliberation, as if the play on words had just occurred to him, he went to the microphone and said, 'You are the living Church of Liverpool,' They cheered loudly and he repeated the phrase several times. Then, unable to resist it any longer, and to the consternation of the special police, present for his security, he dived into their midst, linked arms with some deliriously happy youngsters and joined in to sing 'Bind us together in love'.

We may safely assume that the Pope knew nothing of that small tidal creek on the banks of the River Mersey, which originally provided the natural harbour and which became known as 'The Pool'. Still less will he have heard of the lichen-like weed which made the water sluggish and which centuries ago led the locals to speak of the 'liver' or 'lever' pool. As for the liver-birds, it is generally acknowledged that these largely mythical cormorants are unlikely ever to have seen the inside of an egg-shell. Despite all this, Pope John Paul was right to identify Liverpool with life, and to recognise the vibrant nature of the young people's faith.

It is my belief that this applies to all generations of Liverpudlians and not just to the youth of today. In our book, *Better Together*, Bishop David Sheppard and I wrote: 'Whether we call this phenomenon our unconscious faith or a feeling after God, a rumour of God or an echo of his voice, there seems little doubt that some toe-hold of faith and Christian values remains. The Church is very blind if it dismisses all this as mere superstitious "folk" religion. In many deprived areas, shared hardships and discrimination can produce a remarkable degree of solidarity. Being "members one of another" becomes a living reality in such circumstances. The people know how to respond together to injustice, grief and joy. In face of a crisis, especially where a child is concerned, their generosity and support are immediate. Yet such people are often not on parish electoral rolls or visiting lists. They will often be hesitant, if not actually reluctant, to admit to having a faith. Somehow they see little connection between their faithful ways and what they understand as the formal teaching or disciplines of the institutional Church.'

Since writing about this 'almost unconscious faith', which at other times I have described as incoherent or inarticulate, I have often been asked to explain what we meant. In some ways it would be easier to write a more fully developed treatise for theologians, yet it is my belief that many Liverpool people exemplify what we meant every day of their ordinary lives. They do so in their daily circumstances just as effectively and as often as they reveal it in their worship and church devotions, real and moving though the latter can be. In fact they reveal it in what I believe the Pope glimpsed as he passed through the streets of Liverpool and spoke of the living faith of the young people.

This book is an attempt to give some picture of that living faith. It is a small attempt to close the gap between profound theological writing and the joys and sorrows, the enduring relationships and crisis situations, which mark the commitment of ordinary people in this city to what really amounts to gospel-teaching. Because it is a natural trait, it is seldom openly self-conscious. For obvious reasons names of persons and places have been changed, sometimes only thinly disguised, yet this has enabled me to cast my reminiscences into the form of parables. But they are parables about real people and are drawn from real life.

All the incidents and conversations are firmly based on reality. The journalist in me has allowed very occasional 'poetic licence', and in a few cases I have combined incidents for ease of telling. Generally speaking, the result is a series of living Liverpool parables about the lives, character and faith of real people with whom I have been privileged to spend the last fifteen years and more, and for whom I have the greatest respect and affection.

In no sense does this small book set out to be autobiographical, though in treating the parables I have not hesitated to enter into them in the same way as I have been involved in the incidents and conversations upon which they are based. To have done otherwise could have been unfair and even patronising towards people whose faith has been a great strength to me over the years. Nor is the selection of subjects in any sense comprehensive.

The ecumenical dimension is barely touched upon, and this is because the parables often relate to the sacramental life of the Roman Catholic community. Let me say that the faith of members of other Christian communities has on many occasions also been a source of encouragement and inspiration.

Each of the parables related is followed by a long prayer which takes the form of a meditation or reflection or conversation with God about the incidents I have just related. In one sense this is the easiest and most natural form of prayer, drawn from the reality of the conditions in which we try to work out our salvation.

In preparing these parables and prayers, I have had the encouragement of the members of the Pastoral Formation Team of the Archdiocese of Liverpool, who have hoped that in particular this book may be of help to the many 'eucharistic ministers', commissioned to take Holy Communion to the sick and house-bound. Often these good men and women remain for a while with those they are visiting to help them in prayers of thanksgiving. If my efforts prove of help in such circumstances, they will have been doubly worthwhile.

To a great extent this little book of parables and prayers has been got together during my travels in many parts of this country and abroad during the past year. In a couple of cases the parable relates to incidents about which I have already written an article. It was because of the latter that I began the book, but the treatment of a theme close to my heart is original, just as the lessons of such living faith seem inexhaustible. I have had throughout the help of Mgr John Furnival, my chaplain, and Patricia Jones of the Pastoral Formation Team. Tom Murphy of the *Catholic Pictorial*, has been tireless in securing suitable photographs. To use a Liverpool phrase which you will find often in these pages, with all that the three of them stand for in our 'living Church of Liverpool', I am 'made up'.

+DEREK WORLOCK

Liverpool, June 1991

Dear Lord, incarnate son of Mary,
you were born in a stable.
You know.
Today so many of your people
face great problems and difficulties.
There is a real challenge to their faith.
Give them the resources they need,
as well as the gift of perseverance,
when they feel frustration.
As they fall victim to circumstances not of
   their making,
give them the courage and the desire
to keep on looking for the way forward.
Grant them the advice and help they need
to fulfil your purpose.

I
Welcome

'I hope you've got your old shoes on', said the young priest as we set out to visit some of his house-bound parishioners. It was the first official parish visitation which I had carried out since my transfer from a southern, mostly rural diocese to a northern, highly urban archdiocese. All these years later I will admit that I was anxious to impress upon this post-Vatican II product of the archdiocesan seminary that, though new in Liverpool, I was not without experience.

I looked down intently at my feet and gave him my verdict. 'Strong but comfortable', I assured him, as much as to say that I would still be standing when he was sagging at the knees. But that was not what he had meant.

'No,' he responded, kindly enough. 'It's just that we're going to the "Bully" and sometimes the paint isn't dry.'

Already I had learned the local habit of what was called 'diddymisation': taking the first syllable of the word and adding the letter y. Hence the Scouser would smoke his 'ciggy', eat his 'butty', and drink his 'bevvy'. The 'Bully' was the Bull-ring, a large circular tenement building, five storeys high, with all entrances into the enclosed space in the middle.

As may be imagined, community life was intense. All family and neighbourly relationships were lived in public. There could be few secrets. It provided housing for about 200 families. Solidly built in brick and concrete, it might have resembled a fortress but for the ease of exchange between the residents and the freedom of space on each landing, impeded only by the washing, usually staggered throughout the week.

An archiepiscopal visit would inevitably bring many of the residents to their doorways and landings. A stronghold of the faith, my passage would invite encouragement and advice as to who should or should not be visited.

'Try the next one up, Your Grace. She's poorly.'

'What do you mean about the paint?' I asked my companion who was clearly intent upon en-suring that my experience of visiting that part of our city should be total.

'Well, it all depends on when they had it finished', he replied. 'You'll probably find they have painted the drain-pipes "shocking" purple. Whatever you do, even if it looks dry, don't catch hold of one. Greeting people with a purple hand will be a poor substitute for letting them kiss your ring.'

So I had a humorist on my hands as well. 'And my shoes?' I asked. 'They also paint the treads of the stairs,' he said, 'usually white, sometimes yellow and white – the papal colours,' he added. The man was a mass of information. 'But step right over the doorstep. The "welcome" on the mat is nearly always still wet.'

I looked again at my muddy shoes, and even more anxiously at the hem of my cassock. It sounded as though this would finish up more like

17

Joseph's technicoloured dreamcoat. But more was to come.

'I hope that you won't mind the graffiti,' observed my young companion, also intent upon drawing on experience. 'It doesn't mean much nowadays.' He need not have been over-anxious. The enthusiasts had been out obliterating or rendering sanctimonious the various messages, slogans, directions and occasional profanities, which had enlivened the walls alongside the stairways I was likely to use.

As we emerged on to the landing of the third floor, I was confronted with lettering almost a foot high. GOD BLESS OUR CANON, it proclaimed. 'That's been there since Canon Doyle's golden jubilee,' I was told. 'The whole place was hung with bunting. That was when the old Pro-Cathedral was still up and he was the Administrator. They keep that there to remind them of the good old days.'

'How do they feel about the Cathedral, now they've got it?' I asked.

'Oh, they're very proud of it,' the young priest replied. 'They saved up so much for so long,' he added, 'that even though they got a shock with the design, they resented very much any mention of "Paddy's Wigwam". There's even GOD BLESS OUR CATHEDRAL over there,' he pointed. 'It's almost in self-defence. I think it was first put up after someone from the Lodge got in and painted up some crack about the Mersey Funnel, and

18

whether we had to pay toll to go in. They didn't like that.'

We paused on the landing to look around us. Already the news was out and the landings were filling to get a view of the new 'Arch'. 'A lot of the widows in the "Bully" and in the other buildings round here gave their wedding rings to the Cathedral to be melted down for the gold chalice used for the opening Mass,' the priest told me. 'There weren't many savings left by the time the Cathedral was finished.'

I stepped forward to wave at the women who had gathered over on the far side of the building. They waved back at once and turned to ex-

change comments which mercifully I could not hear.

We moved on towards a festooned doorway which was clearly my immediate destination. It was dripping with wet paint, still running across the floor. The representatives of at least three generations had gathered inside, where in the corner chair was waiting a house-bound parishioner with a double claim to fame. Not merely had he been a brick-layer for the Lutyens crypt upon which the Gibberd super-structure of the new Cathedral had been built; but his proudest boast was that as a young man in a neighbouring parish, he had once carried Archbishop Downey's train – the lengthy *cappa magna* worn by the archbishops of old, in more triumphalist days when they presided in style at a throne.

A small photograph, duly framed, of himself in his cassock and surplice, stood on the mantel-piece as proof of his claim: almost a proclamation of his orthodoxy. I expressed my admiration, and out popped the inevitable question. 'What do you think of Liverpool?'

Already I knew that this polite enquiry could also be a catch question, best not answered, as it often led to the more treacherous slopes of loyalty to one or other of the football teams. So I quickly asked the sick man how long he had been living there, and in no time we were lost in the reminiscences and ramifications of the various generations of which he seemed to be patriarch.

Then he looked anxious, lest we be lost in trivialities. 'You understand, Your Grace, that I can't get out to Mass,' he said. 'I miss that. They bring me holy communion, but I loved my church and I miss that.' I tried to console him about an understanding God. Then we prayed together and I moved to the door. As soon as I appeared in the doorway, shouts went up from the flats on the far side of the Bull-ring. I was being advised, if not actually instructed, to ring two doors along on the same floor.

There stood a fairly formidable lady, arms akimbo, apparently more concerned to greet me than to admit me to her home. 'Go on, Nell,' called a voice from across the Bull-ring, 'bring her out. Ask him for his blessing.' I looked as non-committal as I could manage, but the instruction was ignored. As the cry confirmed, 'Go on, bring her out,' I eventually asked, 'Is there someone else I should see?'

'Only my grand-daughter,' said the one I gathered was Nell, 'and she's expecting.' I asked if I could see her and in no time she had appeared in the doorway, behind her grandmother. There was no doubt that it was she, very obviously expecting.

Immediately the cries from across the way were resumed. 'Nell, get a blessing for the baby. Go on. Your Grace, put your hand on her.' Apparently the royal gift of touch was also expected of me. Inevitably a holy hush fell upon the entire area, as we prayed that the one-parent family due in a matter of days might grow in faith and in health and with the love and support of the local community...

The years go by. That was nearly 15 years ago and only a few weeks ago, in one of the parishes in a perimeter estate, that same child, now a husky lad, was presented to me for confirmation. His mother, now married and with her husband in attendance, reminded me without embarrass-ment of our earlier encounter. Her grandmother, Nell, had by now gone to God. The young moth-er's marriage, though somewhat belated, had been happy. Her husband had a job, and her son was bright.

'It just shows you what a blessing in the "Bully" can do,' she laughed, and I wondered if she had heard some of the advice called out to me before she had found her way to the door.

We talked about the Bull-ring today, of the recent attempts to scatter the residents and de-molish the buildings. More than 100 of the fami-lies had refused to move because they did not wish their community to be broken up. So far they had successfully defied the 'Corpy'. There was a chance that they might all be re-housed nearby but their present conditions with limited services were bad. Incredibly it had been discov-ered that the 'Bully' is a listed building, safe from the planners and the bulldozers. Now there was talk of a Government grant.

'Do you remember all the paint?' I asked her, looking down almost unconsciously at my shoes. 'Yes,' she replied, 'but they don't do that any more in the parish where we live now.' She paused and then gave me her verdict. 'It's a shame really.'

Lord God of power and might,
have compassion on your people,
especially the elderly and the deprived
who know that you are almost the only object of
    their love
that cannot be taken away from them.
Sustain them in their life together,
that in their community
they may find what it means to be
the family of God.

Help them to preserve
the priorities of their faith
and the true values of their homes
and working life.
And as they treasure the heritage of their past,
give them the encouragement they need
to find fulfilment
in the challenges of their today
and faithful hope in their future.

Dear Lord, incarnate son of Mary,
you were born in a stable.
You know,
today so many of your people
face great problems and difficulties.
There is a real challenge to their faith.
Give them the resources they need,
as well as the gift of perseverance,
when they feel frustration.

As they fall victim to circumstances not of their
    making,
give them the courage and the desire
to keep on looking for the way forward.
Grant them the advice and help they need
to fulfil your purpose.

Just now, Lord,
the great word of this decade
seems to be 'empowerment'.
Empower your people
so that they may be a sign of gospel values:
that they may achieve
a home life which is happy and healthy,

and a working life which accords
with the dignity which is theirs
because they are your people.

Dear Lord, good shepherd and true guide,
grant your special protection to the young ones,
who, knocked over by the upheavals of life today,
feel no restraint or hesitation
in kicking over the traces.
For they recognise no purpose
in all the cautions of the past.
When all the supports and ambitions we knew
fail to attract or inspire young people,
help them to find stability and strength
in the knowledge of your love
and in the practice of their faith.

Let them know the joy of the faith they
    have inherited,
and enable them to find and play their rightful
    role
in the local community
and in their parish.
Help them to feel needed
and to know that they belong.
For they are yours, Lord,
and we are yours.
Grant true unity to your people.

Help us to build up your Kingdom
in the Bull-ring and tower-blocks and tenements.
Let your priests be so involved in the life of the
*   parish*
that, just as they are recognised at your altars,
so may they be known and welcomed into the
*   homes of their people.*
Grant that the priests may feel valued,
and that the people may have confidence
in the love and concern
of those who minister to them
in your holy Name. Amen.

And what of the 'left-behind'?
The 'nans' and the grand-dads,
who have had to watch their kith and kin
seek livelihood and prosperity elsewhere?
Are they, as a geriatric generation,
to be written off as redundant,
deprived even of the opportunity
to pass on their most precious gift
of experience and faith?

II
The
Left-behind

'I'm afraid that I can't get up,' said the stout old lady, lying on the couch, rather like an out-size tortoise on its back. 'I don't seem to have any more fight left in me, and just lately my legs have gone.'

It was a Sunday afternoon and I was out on a round of visits to the house-bound in one of the inner city parishes. It had a disproportionate number of those whom the experts called 'the left-behind'. Their families had for the most part been moved out some years ago to the concrete jungles on the outskirts of the city. The same experts call these 'the perimeter estates'.

Gasping with the effort she was making to sit up, the old lady tried to apologise. Clutching the inadequate blanket about her, she was set on making me understand that she had not always been like that.

'I managed to go out to work till I was 80,' she added, in a mixture of pride and self-defence.

She had worked as a cleaner in a hospital until she was 60. Then she was stood off to make room for a younger woman. Her friends had given her a party but there had been no presentation clock. In any case she had to get another job. She had transferred her services as a cleaner to some city offices. That had meant going out each morning at 5 a.m. It was this she had managed to keep up until she was 80.

She turned her sad brave eyes towards me. Who knows what pain and faith lay behind her words? 'I've had a hard life, Father.' It was a statement of fact, rather than a complaint. Then she went on to tell me about her family. She had married a soldier at the end of the First World War. He had been gassed at the Battle of the Somme and never really worked after he was put out of the Army. She bore him eight children before being left a widow in the early 1930's. With remarkable long suffering charity she explained to me that he had not been able to hold down a job and that he drank to excess. Even before he had died, she had had to go out to work in order to provide for her children.

I looked across to the mantelpiece at the faded sepia photographs, with one of her soldier hus-

band in uniform, and presumably some of her grandchildren in their first holy communion outfits.

'Where are they all today?' I asked.

There was one daughter living in an estate some way out of the city, she told me. She could not come in often as she had no transport and bus fares were so heavy now. But this daughter had a fine boy who came in to see his 'Nan' most Sundays.

Then there was a son, now just retiring, living somewhere in the south. She couldn't remember exactly where but she heard from him at Christmas each year. Another of the daughters had married and had lived not far away, but her husband had left her and she too had to get a job. It must have been too much for her as she had died some years later. There had been something in the paper about it...

Of course they were all good children really but they had their own families now, so they could not get to see her very often. Not much change out of eight, I thought; but she went on to explain that a couple of the boys had gone to Australia and lost touch. She had heard that one of them was dead but had no real means of knowing, as they had never written home much.

Her great help was her friend next door. She was very good to her and did what shopping she needed. And there was a home-help who came in most days. Perhaps she would feel stronger when the summer came, though the trouble with the flats was the lift and with her leg trouble she could not manage the stairs.

It was just that the weekends and the nights seemed so long. But, she said almost apologetically, she had never missed Mass on a Sunday until her back and her legs had given out. Nor had she ever smoked or had a drink. 'I couldn't afford it, Father.'

A litany of reminiscences, which added up to hard-won sanctity, arose from the couch. Would I leave her door-key on the string in the letter-box, she asked, just in case her grandson was able to travel in to see her later on? He was unemployed at the moment and sometimes liked to talk over his problems with her.

As we prayed together before I left, I found myself earnestly asking the Lord to make sure that the grandson found a job, a real job, close at hand. More than the latch-key seemed to hang on the end of that string.

Dear Father of the 'left-behind',
look with love on your elderly children,
whose families,
for whom they sacrificed so much,
have moved into seeming oblivion.

Surely the planners did not mean
to deal so harsh a blow,
when they sought to wipe out
the hideous over-crowding of the past.
Did no one foresee the consequences
of scattering these pockets of people
whom we recognise now as 'community'?

The solidarity, which was their strength,
was not just a matter of numbers.
Their strength lay in the family,
a network of human relationships,
more numerous and complex than could be
    packed
into those wretched little boxes
which add up to high-rise buildings.
Yet these were the bait
held out to the desperate,
seeking family accommodation
in a flat with a view
across a barren green-field site.

It sounded great, Lord:
God's fresh air and a chance of a decent living.
But quickly the jobs in the area dried up,

and our young people were encouraged
to 'get on their bikes' –
if they were any good.

Is that all mindless politicians cared
for our values and traditions?

Dear Lord, are such journeys really necessary?
It breaks our hearts to see them go:
not to be able to stem
this haemorrhage of our youth.
And when some of them return,
jobless and dispirited,
having sold their bikes to get back home:
what then, Lord?

And what of the 'left-behind'?
The 'nans' and the grand-dads,
who have had to watch their kith and kin
seek livelihood and prosperity elsewhere?
Are they, as a geriatric generation,
to be written off as redundant,
deprived even of the opportunity
to pass on their most precious gift
of experience and faith?

Lord, sustain the faith and hope
of those who wait alone.
Reward their courage,
heal their hurt.

For all they wanted
was that their children might have
a better chance in life.

For generations we have struggled
to uphold the dignity of human labour.
But without employment to earn a wage
and the respect that goes with it,
where is the dignity
which seems tied to a job?

Lord God of justice and compassion,
help us to overcome bitterness of heart,
and to sustain in faith
those who await
without much hope,
the opportunity of a decent job.

III
Black Friday

'It's another Black Friday, I'm afraid,' said the radio reporter, phoning through to see if I had heard the announcement of yet one more factory closure. The phrase he used was not intended to have any connection with Good Friday: merely a reference to the day of the week on which bad news of this kind is customarily released.

'The embargo is for midday,' he informed me, 'but I wondered if you would like to make a comment right away.' There had been rumours about a closure for some months. Someone had spotted that none of the firm's considerable prof-

its were being ploughed back into the local business. They had been diverted towards the installation of new technology in another factory of the same company near the mouth of the Channel Tunnel.

It was evidently only a matter of time. Earlier that morning there had been a confidential letter from the Management and a phone call from the shop stewards. Both said the same thing: 'Can you help?'

The choice of Friday for the announcement was no accident. When the release of informa-

tion is made at midday, it is already conveniently too late for the evening papers. Next morning, being a Saturday, the Press would be so dominated by sport that even serious bad news would be crowded out of the news columns.

This was the usual pattern, to which we had become accustomed. Losing a thousand jobs is serious bad news for a whole area as well as for the individuals involved. But the truth was that much of the steam would have gone out of the situation by Monday.

Could I help? To the Management that meant an attempt to keep up the morale of the work force whilst the run-down of the factory took place. To the Unions and the work force it meant a struggle to save some jobs from the wreckage – a cut-back rather than a closure – or at least improved redundancy terms.

Within hours of such an announcement certain stances are regularly adopted. 'Our decision is final and irrevocable,' says the spokesman for the Management. That is a deliberate attempt to discourage anyone from hoping for effective negotiation.

'Disgusting,' says the Union convenor. 'We will call out our supporters and sympathisers in branches all over the country. We are not prepared to surrender a single job. If necessary, we shall arrange for a boycott of all the firm's products.'

'It's all due to the chip,' says one of the more

knowledgeable. 'That's the trouble with multi-nationals,' says another. 'The decision was taken in Zurich or Detroit, without thought or knowledge of the local community here.'

'It's very sad,' confides one of the women employees to my friend, the radio reporter, who has taken up his position at the factory gates. 'I've worked at this place for nearly thirty years,' she adds, 'and they always seemed a decent firm too.'

As if in support of her sympathetic statement, the company's Public Relations man, who has made a special journey from Head Office in London to offer consolation, announces officially: 'We shall do everything possible to relocate all those who have to look for other semi-skilled employment elsewhere.' Few find reassurance in this undertaking.

'Don't talk to us about mobility of labour,' says the father of a large family, whose eldest is due to take his GCSE in the summer. 'You can't expect me to tear up my roots here and tout my services around some other part of the country where they want 'season' workers. What about my family? They're entitled to a proper home base.'

'The Management of a company must think about its shareholders,' says the Chairman of the Directors. 'Stop this whingeing. The world does not owe you a living, you know. We have to slim down our operation, to remain competitive.'

So it goes on. Local councillors call for concerted action from all parties. Central government looks the other way, and the Speaker of the House of Commons declines the demand for an emergency debate. There is a renewed cry for a greater degree of private sector investment from outside the area.

Desperate dashes are made to London to see the Company's decision makers. They will weigh all the various representations very carefully, but some anxiety is expressed about the sharpness of local protest and reported plans for a protest march. We are reminded that this might prove harmful to the image of the whole area.

The protest march turns out to be a Good Friday Walk of Witness, which will pass by the gates of the shortly-to-be-abandoned factory. As I walk slowly with the local clergy past the threatened building, I explain to the parish priest that the outcome of my efforts is likely to fall far short of the expectations of the local work force.

'Don't worry,' he replies patiently, 'I understand. The thing is to help these poor people to see the link between their situation today and Good Friday on Calvary.'

Dear Lord, Redeemer of the world,
please help us to understand
how we are expected to make this Black Friday
Good.
Is this really our way of the Cross,
your way of the Cross for us?
Is this how we are to share
in your work of redeeming the world?

We know, from the prophet Isaiah,
that our thoughts are not your thoughts,
our ways are not your ways.

But have we got it all wrong, Lord?
Surely you did not mean
that the wonders of technology
should be used to cut back all these jobs,
and cause this hardship and distress.
As things are just now,
lost jobs can make your marvels
seem like a curse upon your people.

For a very long time, Lord,
we have desired that your working people
should have the time and freedom
to admire and enjoy
the beauty of your creation.
We have longed that they should have lifted from
them
the drudgery of so much of their work.
But it all looks a little different
when seen with the eyes of the unemployed.

What rose-tinted hope
can you bring, Lord,
to their embittered vision?

For generations we have struggled
to uphold the dignity of human labour.
But without employment to earn a wage
and the respect that goes with it,
where is the dignity
which seems tied to a job?

Lord God of justice and compassion,
help us to overcome bitterness of heart,
and to sustain in faith
those who await
without much hope,
the opportunity of a decent job.

Help us to be sensitive
to the blow to pride
and to the self-respect
of a work force cast into redundancy.

Help us to convince
those who look on,
incredulous and critical;
help them to understand that worker-solidarity
is rooted in mutual concern:
not fodder for a strike-weapon,
but a sign of membership
of your One body.

Dear Father God,
you loved your people so much
that you sent your only Son
to share our lives
and be our Saviour.
Just for a few days,
at Christmas time,
our world slows down
enough for us to celebrate –
in some sort of way –
the birthday of Jesus
and his coming amongst us.

IV

Celebrating Christmas

The famine-relief carol was top of the charts. 'Do they know it's Christmas?' seemed likely to displace 'Once in Royal David's city'. In a secular but generous world, used to fulfilling its charitable responsibilities through tax-relief and telethons, the focus had shifted from the Holy Land to Ethiopia.

As I made my way into a primary school in the heart of the city, it occurred to me that to ask the pupils if they knew it was Christmas time was a little unreal.

There was scarcely a school window which did not bear suitable seasonal greetings. Cut-out figures of Father Christmas, well-rounded snowmen and flourishing fir-trees abounded. The amount of cotton-wool employed must have presented a problem to the Regional Health Authority.

One corridor, festooned with hanging tinsel and almost impassable with an inverted forest of neatly-twisted crepe-paper, set me wondering why the school governors had complained about a shortage of exercise-books.

I made slow progress from the Infants' Reception class to the top Juniors. An infant with a paint-brush and a fine creative spirit revealed to me that she was painting sheep: the shepherds had not yet arrived. With the help of a stencil, stars were being manufactured by the dozen. A small boy, well stuck into his plasticine, was making a birthday-cake for Jesus.

I sat through several performances of 'Little Donkey' and began to develop a marked preference for 'Silent Night', or even 'Feed the world'. I asked the right questions about the Wise Men to enable the star-turn in the class to tell me that among the gifts taken to the manger were a goal and 'frankenstein'.

'The children are all very excited,' the head teacher explained unnecessarily. 'Tomorrow they are doing their play.' I presumed that I was about to see a rehearsal of the end-of-term Nativity Play and I glanced secretly at my watch. 'Which one are they doing?' I enquired anxiously. 'It's a pantomime,' replied the head. 'We've written it ourselves, and it's full of local characters and local jokes. It's become John and the Beanstalk.'

I had my suspicions but decided I had better 'buy it' and ask why. 'The hero is John Barnes,' he said with a rather sick smile. 'Of course, it's the children's choice, not mine. I'm an Evertonian.' He looked lovingly at one of the card board Magi on the wall, who appeared to be wearing a blue scarf.

Rashly I asked the small black lad in front of me what part he was playing in the play. I should have guessed. 'John,' he grinned. 'And what's your real name?' I asked. 'John Paul' was the proud reply. Born in 1982, I thought, at the time of the Papal Visit.

The head's secretary put her head into the class-room and said to him: 'There's a telephone call for you in your office.' 'You had better go and take it,' I said, determined to hold my own. 'It's probably Kenny Dalglish on the phone, wanting to sign him up.'

'Feed the world,' blared out the record player as I left the class room. 'Do they know it's Christmas time?' It seemed a bit unnecessary. On my way out I walked past three life-size paper Magi, heading for Bethlehem.

'There's just one more thing,' said the local priest to whom I had turned to say goodbye in the car park. 'Look, I'm afraid that I'm in a terrible hurry,' I tried to explain, 'there's someone waiting for me at the Cathedral.' 'It's just that there is an old lady who has asked to see you,' he countered. 'I think she's dying and she's no distance away.' 'Is it on the way to the Cathedral?' I asked, rather impatiently. 'Yes,' he lied, as he turned the car in the opposite direction.

The old lady's husband had the door open a few inches, on the security chain, as we arrived. He began a speech of welcome but we hurried upstairs to his wife's bedroom. Somehow she raised herself from her bed of pillows, taking care not to disturb her rosary and last year's Christmas card, laid out with the bottle of Lourdes water on the coverlet.

'I knew you'd come,' she said, reaching out and taking possession of my hand. 'Bless my eyes,' she told me. As I did so, she added, 'I was always taught that priests are God's representatives. So I thought that if I could just hold you for a bit, it might help me with the pain.'

'Do you have a lot of pain?' I asked. 'Oh yes,' was the reply, 'but I musn't complain. I've had a long life. There's many worse off.'

So whilst my appointment waited at the Cathedral we prayed for a while: for her, for her scattered family and the children in the school. Then I saw her fish around under the pillows for her purse. 'No, no,' I said, 'you musn't worry.' 'It's for all those starving people in Ethiopia,' she pleaded.

I did not need the radio to hear the chant this time: 'Feed the world. Do they know it's Christmas?'

They knew all right. The Chancellor of the Exchequer may have curbed their consumerist tendencies in the big stores, but the young and the old people, even those who doubt if they have a faith, knew all right about Christmas.

They knew that it was the birthday of the one who came to share their sorrows and their joys. Christ incarnate in their lives.

Dear Father God,
you loved your people so much
that you sent your only Son
to share our lives
and be our Saviour.
Just for a few days,
at Christmas time,
our world slows down
enough for us to celebrate –
in some sort of way –
the birthday of Jesus
and his coming amongst us.

Help us, throughout the year,
amidst all our busy-ness,
to remember his presence in our lives.

So much lies behind that word
INCARNATION:
his taking of human flesh,
body and blood,
from the one whom he gave to us
as our mother.

Mary could truly say of him,
'Flesh of my flesh';
and by the Incarnation,
Lord, you have made him our brother.
But for your word
it would be incredible.
Help me to accept it,
even when I cannot understand.

As we gather in our homes at Christmas,
amidst so much happiness and feasting,
keep this thought central in our minds:
so that we may remember
whose birthday it is,
and why it's a celebration for <u>all</u> your family
worldwide.

Great efforts are made each year
to bring happiness to children
at this time.
But, Father, we are all your children.
Guide us as we seek
to extend the generosity
of our giving, our caring, our love,

to the deprived and the disabled,
to the homeless and the uncared-for,
to the unloved
and those whom we find it hard to like.

Bless the parents and teachers
who each year seek new ways
to put flesh on the Christmas story.
Strengthen those who at this time
must carry the genuine burdens of this world.

From the pain and stress incurred
in bringing your Son's message of peace
into the world,
ease us with the joy
of a new child in our home;
and lift our hearts
with the new hope and ideals,
which your tender infant son
brings to us who remember.

Make us patient with those
who do not know about Christmas.
Give us new zeal and urgency
in proclaiming the message
of the herald angels.
And when we get carried away, Lord,
with the gifts and good wishes
which by rights are your Son's,
freshen our memories, dear Lord,
with what it's all about.

Help us to recognise your presence
in the seeming crises
that rack our daily lives.
Give stability to our faith
so that our hearts and home
may be your dwelling-place.

And, by the way, Lord,
forgive us if at times your sheep
do too much bleating.

V
'The Sheppy'

'They can't just shut it,' said the local supporter defiantly. 'I've paid up something every week of my life; 5p or 10p a week lately.' 'That's right,' agreed his wife. 'Whenever we've gone for treatment, we've always put something in the collecting box. And when we were kids, we used to go out collecting on a Saturday morning.'

Their reaction to the reports that 'The Sheppy' might have to close was understandable, typical and inevitable. For the Good Shepherd Voluntary Hospital was so much a part of their lives that any threat to its continued existence was unthinkable.

'Whose hare-brained idea to close it, is it anyway?' they asked angrily. 'It's not fair on the nuns after all these years. Reverend Mother won't agree to it, you may be sure of that. In any case it's no time since we had that Centenary Appeal.'

An immediate approach to the Town Hall found the Mayor only too willing to make a formal statement: '"The Sheppy" has a unique place in the affections of all our citizens. It is a memorial to our past and an inspiration for our future. Someone has made a mistake somewhere.'

The local newspaper re-set its front page. 'Save our Sheppy' was the obvious headline. It had all started as a hideous rumour, but now the report was confirmed. It was understood that serious consideration was being given to the proposed closure by the hospital's trustees.

'Who are these faceless men?' the newspaper demanded, much to the embarrassment of the nuns themselves who knew that in fact the trustees were their own Religious Superiors.

Some luckless local councillor made himself few friends by suggesting to the newspaper reporter that the story was just a gimmick to boost support for the Centenary Appeal which so far had met with little success.

He should have known better. As a member of the local Health Authority, he must have been well aware of the crippling cost of maintaining and equipping a general hospital today. Already his committee had had to seek an estimate for updating the equipment installed in the Operating Theatre and Radiology Department, built only 10 years earlier. But this was not the only problem facing the trustees. Their Order of nursing Sisters had fallen in numbers. There were not enough trained and qualified Sisters available now to fill the key nursing posts in the hospital.

The salaries needed to employ professional nurses as replacements for retired Sisters made the contributions in the collecting boxes in 'Casualty' even more inadequate.

What about help from the local Health Authority? With new building and the steady development of provision by the National Health Authority, their need to use 'pay beds' in the 'Sheppy' had almost ceased.

With obligatory contributions to National Insurance, who could be expected to pay twice? Certainly not the Health Authority.

The Board of Management issued a statement confirming the gravity of the situation but making plain the opposition of its members to the closure of the hospital. The Matron and nursing staff professed their undying loyalty to the institution which was 'the people's friend'. The Medical Committee duly expressed its admiration for the Sisters and its confidence that somehow a way forward would be found.

'The Sheppy' entered its death throes. The expected procedures must be followed.

The Chairman of the Health Authority found a picket on his office doorstep one morning. A delegation waited upon the already sympathetic local Members of Parliament. A deputation of committee members was photographed, boarding the train for London, to have talks with the Mother General of the Order, who in any case was due to visit the hospital later that week.

At last, to take the heat out of events, a temporary solution was found. A Working Party was established: to examine the situation and make recommendations. Its findings were foreseeable, but at least its slow deliberations provided time for people to come to terms with the inevitable.

Once it was clear that there was no alternative use for the hospital's redundant buildings, all interest was in the site. It was here that the Sisters declared themselves.

Even if there were industrial concerns interested in the commercial development of the site, the nuns remained determined that at least in part the site should be used in some way for the benefit of the local community. 'The Sheppy' had served the health needs of the people in the past. Somehow its value must be preserved and related to the future needs of those living in the locality.

There was a long and painful period of uncertainty, marked by vigils, protests, farewells and thanksgivings. But by the time the bulldozers had done their work, an agreement had been reached with a housing association for the building of sheltered housing for the elderly: the beneficiaries would be those for whom 'The Sheppy' had been a landmark in their lives.

Opening ceremonies for sheltered housing schemes can often be unsatisfactory, in that the new home occupiers have not always settled into their new surroundings. But such was not the case when the opening of the new 'Sheppy Village' took place.

With many of those who had been concerned in the early months of crisis, we prayed that those now placed in the new flats and houses would enjoy the same love and care as they had known from the Good Shepherd Hospital. The Sisters seemed delighted. The Mayor and the Health Authority seemed delighted. A number of official representatives made suitably envious remarks.

What about the new residents? We set out on a tour of those selected for a visit. This was to be the real test.

When accompanied by an official visiting party of this kind, I always hang back when the group moves out in case the residents want to tell me something without the others knowing. On this particular round, the residents ensured that this was the case.

There were special things to be said. Most of the residents were from the streets round about the old 'Sheppy'. They all seemed 'made up' with their new homes. And if they were not well or needed help, there was a warden available on the end of the bell.

The nicest surprise came near the end of the

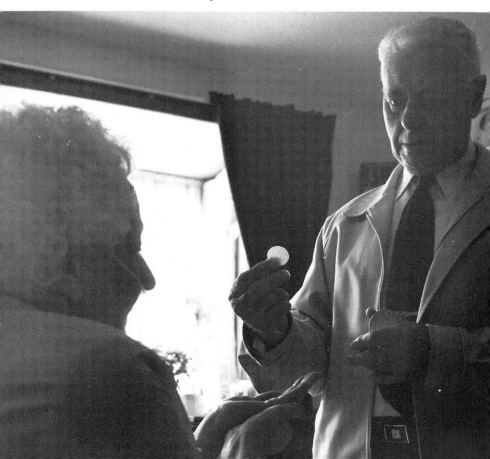

round. I was conscious of being hijacked by an elderly couple who couldn't wait to get the others out of their home. Then the husband stood before me to announce: 'I thought you ought to know. I'm a eucharistic minister.'

'Fine,' I replied. 'How long is it since you were commissioned?' 'About three years,' he said, 'but I only began properly when we moved in here. Before that I just helped in Church on Sunday.'

I asked him to tell me more.

'Well,' he said, 'I'm still pretty good on my legs and can get to St Pat's for the 9 o'clock each morning. But the wife can't manage it. So I bring her back holy communion like she used to have at daily Mass when she was well.'

As the old lady thanked God for this great privilege, her husband went on: 'In fact, Father lets me cover all the people in the "Sheppy Village", as they call it. He's on his own now, and it would be too much for just one priest because he's got lots of other people to get round. But I make sure they all have communion here if they can't get across to church – and several times a week, if they want.'

He told me how years before he had been a hospital porter, and I thought of all the hospital chaplains he would have known, who served the 'Sheppy' in the past. Together the three of us knelt down and thanked the Good Shepherd for the enrichment he had given to the loving care of his people.

Dear Lord,
You are all things to us:
so we address you
with many different titles
according to our needs.

When we call you our Good
*   Shepherd,*
it is because we remember
what Jesus called himself.
He described himself like that
because that was how he knew
and cared for his flock.
He said that it was also
how we, his sheep, would
*   know him.*

*It is for your care and guidance
that we turn to you now.*

*Help us to listen
to the calls and directions you give us,
so that we may find our way
to your heavenly pastures
where you will give us repose.*

*Help us to stay
within those paths of righteousness
where we shall know
your goodness and mercy.
O best of all shepherds,
you share the crook of your pastoral care
with your bishops.*

Give them strength and
*   gentle authority,*
and a voice of faith and leadership
that all may recognise.

Today, especially,
their task is to be eased
by the zeal and example
of members of their flock.
But it is not always easy, Lord.
So help us to be patient,
to be understanding,
to respond and be enriched,
as we try to make each new change
an opportunity for grace.

You have given us the Church,
and the tradition of the apostles,
to guide us in our belief.
But sometimes we become
so concerned and worried
with the maintenance of our inheritance
and with the fabric of our buildings,
that we forget the mighty span
of the mission you have left
to the flock who follow you.

Cherishing our traditions
and the faith of our fathers,
we are not always ready
for the challenge of these times.

Fearful of what seems different,
we close our minds
to the deep meaning of the new ways
through which you reveal yourself to us.
Give us the courage and the vision
to follow you
in these as yet untrodden paths.

Help us to recognise your presence
in the seeming crises
that rack our daily lives.
Give stability to our faith
so that our hearts and homes
may be your dwelling-place.

And, by the way, Lord,
forgive us if at times your sheep
do too much bleating.

We know our dependence on you.
Please understand
that we are not complaining:
it is just our way of asking.
And, Lord,
you did tell us to ask.

Reward with your grace
the renewed and energetic zeal of those,
who, for the sake of your people,
have embarked upon
what the world would call
'a second career'.
May it also prove to be
a means of helping young people
to a new evaluation
of a nun's vocation.
We praise you, Lord,
for this enrichment of the religious life
and of the service offered in the parishes.

VI
The
Flutter

'It's given me a new start, a second life,' said the Parish Sister who was taking me round to visit some of the house-bound in her district of St Augustine's parish. 'You see, I had been teaching in school for nearly 30 years, and I was looking forward to retirement.'

She checked her list of names and addresses and then went on to explain: 'I was scared at the prospect of spending the rest of my days in a community of elderly and retired Sisters. Anyhow, I didn't feel that I was ready to be put on the shelf, even though I had had enough of the class-room.'

Her reaction to her new task was welcome but not unusual. But quite evidently she had made up her mind to tell me how she had found herself at 'St Gussie's'.

I nodded to her to go on, since I needed to try to save my breath as she hurried me along, threading her way knowledgeably amongst the various blocks of flats in what was generally accepted to be an urban priority area.

'It's three years ago since our Provincial Council,' she explained, 'when our Superiors agreed to set up an experimental small community to work as parish sisters in some needy area.' I remembered the letter telling me of this decision, with the request that I suggest a suitable parish. I had not been too optimistic that the nuns would in fact come, as I knew that the Sister Provincial had at the same time approached three other dioceses.

I had also been quite unwilling to cast any parish into a guinea-pig role and said as much. If the Order wished to join us, I would suggest where. If they wanted, they could have a formal contract with the local parish. But no more experiments, please. Often it was not fair on the people.

In a very business-like way the Superiors agreed. They accepted my straight talk and offered us the services of three Sisters to live in a redundant presbytery. It had been built for four priests in the past. Now there was one. He moved into a small house nearby, previously occupied by the school care-taker. The Sisters arrived to take over the presbytery.

At first the parishioners had been opposed to the proposal. A presbytery was for priests, not nuns. The move seemed a challenge to the future of St Augustine's. Patience was needed. The rightness of the move would only be proved by the character of the Sisters and the value of their work.

It was this which I was witnessing in my round of visits with Sister Mary. But now I was hearing her side of the story.

'I believe there were ten volunteers,' she told me, 'and I never expected to be chosen. When we arrived, I was nervous about the people's reaction. But Father prepared the way for us, and took us to see the sick ones himself, so that they would understand when we came to visit them.'

I hesitated to tell her of his insistence that she accompany me on my official visitation of the sick, rather than he, so as to validate the ever increasing role of the Sisters in the parish. So I asked her to tell me about the next couple we were due to visit.

'Oh, they're both very good,' she said, slipping into a priest's customary easy evaluation, 'but they're not at all well nowadays. I believe that they used to do a lot in the parish in the past. Ted has a very bad heart now, and Kathleen is crippled with arthritis. They're on the ground floor but they're not able to get out to Church.'

She went on to tell me about who did the shopping for them, drew their pensions for them and kept them in touch with the rest of the parish. She had learned the pastoral techniques quickly enough.

We turned into a large block and rang the bell of the ground floor flat. It was the middle of the afternoon and she had told them I would be coming, but no one came to answer the door. Sister Mary became a bit agitated at the delay, and I suggested that if they were as immobile as she said, it would take some time for one of them to get to the door.

'I can't understand it. We're right on time,' she assured me, 'and I told them to leave the door open.' 'Perhaps they have forgotten,' I suggested. She lifted the flap of the letterbox and listened. 'Just what I thought,' she said, 'they've got the television on and they won't hear the door-bell; or else they've both fallen asleep in front of the fire.'

She put her mouth to the letter-box and let out a shout: 'Ted, Kath, it's Sister Mary.' She rattled the flap and then got down to look through it. A look of triumph on her face disclosed the fact that the sitting-room door had opened. 'Is anyone there?' called a woman's voice. 'It's Sister Mary,' went back the reply, 'and I've brought the visitor I told you about.'

Kathleen made her slow painful way to the front-door, drew back the bolts and opened it. 'Sorry, Sister,' she said, 'we thought it was tomorrow you were coming.' She paused. 'Shall I light the candles?' she asked.

'No, I'll come-back and bring you communion tomorrow morning, like I do every Friday. This is our *special* visitor. Remember?'

I was not too sure that she did, but we had gained entry and made our way to the sitting room where Ted was sitting in a high-backed chair opposite the television set. He had the remote control in his hand, but the tell-tale spot of the fading picture, just switched off, still showed in the centre of the screen.

Ted was breathing rapidly, gulping in air and in fairly obvious distress. I remembered being warned that he had a bad heart, so I tried to reassure him by telling him not to move and to take his time. We would sit quietly until he felt better.

'He gets a bit of a flutter sometimes, when he gets excited,' explained Sister Mary. 'Take your time,' I said, 'I'm in no hurry.'

He nodded, apparently grateful for my understanding, but Kathleen soon corrected my grounds for concern. 'It's not you he's excited about, Father. Ted's just had a bit of a shock. It was something he saw on the telly.'

I tried to think what he might have been watching on a Thursday afternoon: a serial or an old film? Then I remembered the sound we had heard through the letter-box, when the wife had opened the living-room door.

'Was it the racing?' I asked with a confident smile, and for the first time Ted managed his own response. 'Yes, Father,' he breathed wheezily. His wife smiled: 'We don't often watch it, Father, but he'd been given a tip and he had a bet on.' 'Did he win?' I enquired without much hope, and again the wheeze came from Ted's chair. 'Yes, Father.'

Sister Mary seemed uncertain whether to try to explain it all away or to congratulate him. More practically, I asked him the name of the horse.

Ted almost choked but managed to get it out at last: 'Be Thankful,' he said, and then added respectfully, 'Father.'

Quite a name for a horse, I thought, and wondered who had given him the tip. As he gradually recovered his breath, I asked him the obvious question: 'And are you thankful, Ted?'

'Oh yes, Father,' he replied without hesitation. 'You see, I've got a good wife and Sister Mary brings us both communion once a week.' Then, having witnessed to his values, he chuckled and choked as he told me, 'Yes, and I was thankful even before I had my little flutter on that horse this afternoon.'

'You and your little flutters,' remonstrated Sister Mary. 'Have the candles ready when I come in the morning, Kathleen,' she added and hurried me on to the next one on her list.

Almighty God and Father,
Lord of all gifts and talents,
we thank you for the generous spirit
and unyielding faith
of so many religious Sisters today.

Reward with your grace
the renewed and energetic zeal of those,
who, for the sake of your people,
have embarked upon
what the world would call
'a second career'.

Source of all true calling,
we thank you also

for the fulfilment they have found
in this new expression
of their vowed commitment.

May it also prove to be
a means of helping young people
to a new evaluation
of a nun's vocation.

We praise you, Lord,
for this enrichment of the religious life
and of the service offered in the parishes.
Please help all those they serve
to overcome first fears
of a second best,
and to recognise instead
this fullness of the Church's ministry.

And, Lord, we praise you
for the enduring faith of your people,
in sickness, deprivation or old age.
May they always enjoy in their needs
the understanding and support of others:
so that they may preserve their sense of dignity
and reasonable independence
within the community.

May there be true appreciation
of their contribution, past and present,
to their neighbourhood and their Church.
Sustain them in their uncertainties

and, as infirmities afflict them,
strengthen their love and their patience
with themselves and one another.

Give them courage
and a sense of security
amidst the threats and challenges
of urban life today.
And help others, who are their neighbours,
to recognise in their example,
not resignation in face of the uncontrollable,
but a living faith
in your presence in their lives.

For, in truth,
to be 'ours' to anyone else
can be but a pale reflection
of what we are to you.
Help us, then, Lord,
not to resist nor resent
being possessed by anyone else
in your name,
and for your sake.
To respond positively
to possession by another
can be very demanding.
A priest is a 'man for others',
like your Son, Jesus Christ.
Help us never to lose
the freedom which comes with generosity,
the unselfish devotion
which flows from priestly service.

VII
'Our' Priest

'That's our priest, Father,' said the enthusiastic lady in the crowd who had come to Lime Street to see her friends off on the annual pilgrimage to Lourdes. She seized my arm and faced me down the platform towards a small group of pilgrims making their way towards us. Evidently they had already handed over their heavy luggage to the couriers near the guard's van; and now laden with a variety of plastic carrier bags, bulging with goods for their journey, they were seeking their places on the train.

'There's Father,' said the lady who had taken possession of my arm, 'that's our priest.' I looked at the bearer of this proud designation and felt glad for him as well as for his parishioners that he had become so much part of their possession. It meant not only that both parties were at home with one another. Their use of 'our' was a fair indication of their understanding and appreciation of the commitment he had made at his ordination.

They might not be able to say much theologically about the sign-value of his celibacy in today's secularist society. They knew that his being their priest had something to do with the totality of God's gift to his servant, and his total gift of himself for the sake of the Kingdom. And to them, that meant them and their parish of Holy Angels.

Completely at ease with this group of his parishioners, the priest gave me a slightly embar-

rassed smile which underwrote the predicament
of his situation. Perhaps some of the embarrass-
ment was due to the travelling mufti he was
wearing and which replaced his customary sombre black. But he grinned more widely as he
lifted aloft a large Bugs Bunny toy belonging to a
small child in his group, and a plastic bag suitably
adorned with a picture of the Cathedral, but from
which protruded soft drinks bottles, bananas,
biscuits and countless packets of 'butties'.

'This belongs to Janie,' he said, perhaps unnecessarily, holding the outsize toy rabbit by the
ears, before tossing it into the carriage. 'Have you
met Janie?' he enquired, calling across to where I

was standing. 'She can't talk yet, but she's brilliant and the pride of the parish. And this is her mother, Anne.' By this time the group were into the carriage, so I went across to talk to them before they set off on the annual adventure of the diocesan pilgrimage to the Shrine at Lourdes.

'Janie,' said the priest to the unsmiling little girl, sitting with her mother in the corner of the compartment, 'say "Hullo" to the Arch.' Dead silence. Quite frankly, she was more interested in the toy rabbit which she had recovered from the rack up above. 'It's our Archbishop, Janie,' said the mother, adding more practically, 'give him your best smile, luv.'

A rather nervous, barely comprehending smile flickered momentarily across the little girl's face. 'Look at that,' said one of the enthusiastic parishioners, 'she's half better already. We'll have her talking by the time we get back, won't we, Janie.' But Bugs Bunny had already regained the child's attention.

'We have the whole parish praying for Anne and Janie whilst they're away,' the priest told me. 'They'll have the best support group in the business.' 'Oh, they've been wonderful,' said the mother. 'As soon as Father had the idea of sending Janie to Lourdes with the pilgrimage, the parish all clubbed together to pay for it and made sure that there was enough for me to come too, to look after her.'

The priest seemed anxious to divert the conversation from his own role. 'Sure, we'll all have a great time together, won't we, Janie,' he said, turning away and whispering to me as he did so. 'The dad's gone off and left them, I'm afraid. The poor lad didn't seem able to take it.'

So the one-parent family settled down for the long journey. As I was leaving the compartment, their priest added, 'I think you know Maureen, don't you, Father.' I looked round and there, smiling before me a great deal more confidently than when last I had seen her, was another woman pilgrim whom I remembered well from the previous year's pilgrimage.

'So you're coming again,' I said, 'I'm so glad. We shall be in Lourdes for the anniversary, won't we? We must try and get Mass together that day.' Her eyes filled as she nodded agreement and added, 'Yes, I'm coming as a helper this year. So is Frank. He's out there now somewhere, helping to load all the suitcases and chairs and medical supplies.' Frank was her husband. We had had to send for him twelve months before when their invalid daughter, whom the mother had taken to Lourdes as a very sick pilgrim, had suddenly taken a grave turn for the worse. It was then that the faith of the parents had shown itself. Nor could I forget the families lining the streets to the parish Church when we had brought the body home for the funeral.

'It was a hard decision to come back this year,' Maureen told me, 'but Father encouraged us to face it as a family. So our boy is with the youth section of the pilgrimage this year, and Frank and I have come as helpers. We've made arrangements to be on duty in the hospital in Lourdes the night of the anniversary of when Carmel died. Father said he would fix it up for us. We thought it would really be the best way of remembering our Carmel and of saying "Thanks" to all the nurses who looked after her and all of us so well'.

Her eyes filled again. So I promised to try to visit them in the ward when they fulfilled their anniversary duty. Then I left the little group to find my own place in the train, near a window in the front carriage from which I could wave 'goodbye' to the stay-at-home relatives and for the benefit of the photographer from the local newspaper.

'Our' priest decided to abandon his flock temporarily in order to walk me to 'our' carriage lest I be waylaid en route by other enthusiastic faithful. 'It looks as though you're in for a busy few days,' I said, and then kicked myself lest he remind me that he had been busy all his life and especially for the nearly 20 years he had been parish priest of Holy Angels. 'Oh, they're a good lot,' he replied generously. I suspected that he was remembering our last conversation some months earlier, when he had come to ask me if I thought he should move as he was running out of ideas. I had told him that if he, or his doctor, thought he should move for health or other reasons, we would look for another post for him at once.

'If not,' I had added, 'I imagine we should think of your people. They have had so many changes in their part of the inner city, due to recession and unemployment, not to mention Vatican II; you're about the only unchanging and stable factor in their lives.' 'I hoped you would say that,' he had replied.

But that morning at Lime Street there was no time for speeches. Just 'Remember what I said. Thank you for agreeing to stay with them. And good luck.' Then 'our' priest went back to his people.

Dear Lord of all
and Father of mankind,
we are nothing
and have nothing
save what comes from you.

Most things of which we speak as 'ours'
we merely hold in stewardship.
But used of people
the word implies relationship,
not possession.
It can even mean 'belonging', Lord,
that cherished word
which means some form of sharing,
making 'yours' and 'theirs'
'ours'.
Let me belong to you, Lord.

When, in obedience to your Son,
we pray 'Our Father',
we cannot strictly claim possession of you,
as if our very will were yours.
Instead we beg your Fatherhood
and claim to be your children,
our relationship enhanced
through Jesus, our brother.

For, in truth,
to be 'ours' to anyone else
can be but a pale reflection
of what we are to you.

Help us, then, Lord,
not to resist nor resent
being possessed by anyone else
in your name,
and for your sake.

To respond positively
to possession by another
can be very demanding.
A priest is a 'man for others',
like your Son, Jesus Christ.
Help us never to lose
the freedom which comes with generosity,
the unselfish devotion
which flows from priestly service.

May our gift of ourselves to your people
help them to understand
that they belong to you:
that you are 'our' God
and that we are all your people.

Lord, this is a priestly prayer,
but may it be prayed too
by your faithful people:
that others may feel able
to respond to your precious call
to service in the priesthood.

Help them to understand
that when their priest,

recognising their needs,
metaphorically or really
takes a towel
to gird himself about his waist,
it is but an extension
to the amice about his neck.

And because we do these things to them,
as we would do it for you, Lord,
and for your sake,
please claim us for your own.
For if we are truly your priests, Lord,
we shall always be 'our priests'
to your people. Amen.

Lord Jesus,
By the Incarnation
and by your coming amongst us,
you brought sanctification
to family life.
Despite the inadequacy of our understanding,
and the pressures of contemporary society,
help us to regain
some of the lost strength
of our nation's family life.
Lord, what would today's statisticians
have made of your family circle
as a social unit?
A one-parent family,
father unknown?
To what social benefits
was St Joseph entitled,
and later his widow,
your mother, Mary,
to whose generous care
you entrusted us?

VIII
'Super-Nan'

'The Americans call it the "hedgehog syndrome",' I said to the priest who was leading me towards a high-rise block of flats in his parish.

'Well, the people don't like it,' he replied. 'They feel stacked on top of one another, and yet there's no real communication.'

'That must be what the Americans mean,' I suggested. 'I suppose the people tuck their heads in and shut out the rest of the world.'

'Roll up into a ball and use their prickles in self-defence,' replied the priest, warming to the idea. 'The higher the rise, the less the communication,' he added. 'Most of the people here hate them. They were moved out here from the old back-to-backs in Scotland Road, and even a generation later they still hanker after the community they knew in the old days.'

We had almost reached the entrance, where a number of children were demonstrating with a tin-can the skills they reckoned 'Rushie' had displayed at Anfield the previous afternoon. Or was it 'Inchy' Heath at Goodison? I knew better than to ask.

'Who are we going to see?' I asked the priest.

'It's an old lady on the 14th floor,' he replied. 'She hasn't been too well lately. She got mugged in her doorway and none of her neighbours heard her cries for help. It's made her nervous.'

'It's my Mum's Nan,' said one of the three small boys who had attached themselves to us, as we waited by the lift. 'Are you the Archbishop?' he

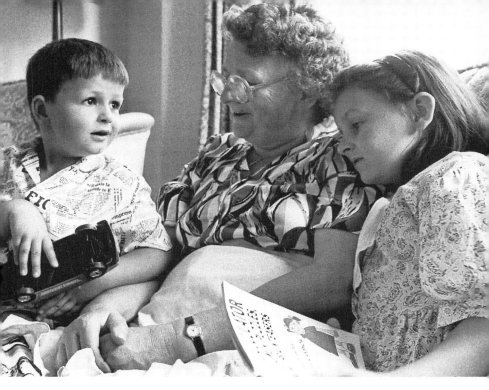

asked. I nodded. 'We call her "Super-Nan" he
confided. 'She's the oldest great-Nan in these flats.'

'Perhaps in the world,' said the smallest excit-
edly.

'How old's that?' asked the priest. But the boys
didn't know. 'She must be pretty old, because
she's my Mum's Nan and my Mum's 28. Grand-
dad told me.'

As the lift bore us up to the 14th floor, the
ramifications of 'Super-Nan's' family tree were
unfolded before me. It represented an extended
family group which, if they could all have been
brought together, would have required a wide-
angle lens of the local photographer.

A representative gathering awaited us in 'Super-Nan's' flat on the 14th floor. Herself, white-haired and frail-looking, sat bolt upright but seeming somewhat bewildered in a high-backed chair, well-stuffed with cushions. A hush fell on the assembly as we were admitted to the presence and introductions were begun.

There was a cluster of O.A.P. daughters, two married grand-daughters and their husbands, and four great-grandchildren, including the three who had broken off their football to be our escort. The four of them were lined up on a settee beside 'Super-Nan's' throne, and on the wall behind them hung several generations of first communion photos.

'How are you, Kitty?' asked my companion who in virtue of his role as parish priest was evidently permitted such familiarity.

'Tell Father how you are, Mum,' said one of the daughters, adding before 'Super-Nan' could get a word in, 'She's better, Father, but she's still not eating properly.'

'I couldn't eat,' said the old lady, 'not for a month. It was the shock. It was my gold cross they took. I didn't mind the money. Oh, Father,' she said, 'it was my fault; I should have kept the door on the chain, like you told me to.'

'Never mind, Nan,' said the grandson-in-law. 'It's all over now.'

But the full story had to be told. Clearly it had been well-rehearsed. The daughters and the grand-daughters knew exactly when to come in with the supplementary questions. The great grand-sons settled down on the settee and munched sweets as they sat contentedly in the front row.

'Tell the Archbishop what they took, Kitty,' demanded the priest, anxious lest this matinee performance should interfere with the schedule of visits he had worked out for me.

Very deliberately, recalling each item on her fingers, 'Super-Nan' recalled the horrid facts. 'They took my poll-tax,' she said, looking at the mantel-piece where presumably she had collected it. 'And they took my water rate' (Pause.) 'They took my money for the African Missions' – 'About £100', explained a daughter. (Further pause)… 'And they took the bits and pieces I had put together to keep handy for the great-grandchil-dren when they come in.'

The munching stopped for a minute so that my young companions might look downcast. 'What else, Nan?' asked their Mum.

The old lady lowered her head, put her hand to her neck and said slowly, and with such reverence that one almost experienced the wound with which the outrage had been perpetrated, 'My gold cross,' she said at last. 'They took my gold cross. I'd had it since I was married. One of the young devils held me down, whilst the other one tore it from my neck.'

The old lady lowered her head in silence and I thought for a moment that she would break down in tears.

'Did you tell the police?' asked the priest.

'They didn't seem interested,' 'Super-Nan' replied. 'More concerned about the cash, they said. Perhaps I should have made more of it, but I was that upset– .'

'We'll have to fix you up with a "mike",' said the daughter who lived in the flat across the landing. 'I never heard a thing,' she added. 'But she was so upset,' she turned towards her mother, 'and you couldn't eat a thing, could you, Mum, not for a whole month. The doctor said it was the shock.'

'Never mind,' said the grandson-in-law, coming to the rescue, 'if you hadn't been unwell, Nan, we might not have got this visit from the Archbishop.'

The old lady pulled herself together. 'Made up,' she said brightly, 'I'm right made up that you should call.' Then: 'And you, Father. It seems a terrible cold afternoon: would you like a drink?' She looked anxiously at her daughters as if they had committed a sin of omission.

We rose hastily, excused ourselves and made for the door.

'Super-Nan' pulled herself up on her feet and managed what came close to being a curtsey. Then the command was given and her children, grand-children and great grand-children slithered down on to their knees. We managed a quick prayer together, and I heard the grandson-in-law whisper, 'Go on, Nan. Ask him.'

'What's that?' I asked the old lady, 'Is there anything I can do for you before I go?'

To her credit she blushed slightly, saying: 'Oh, I don't know. I don't really like to...'

'Come on,' said the priest, 'What do you want him to do? He's got to go on to see some others...'

'She wants you to sign her picture,' said one of the daughters, and I looked round to see who had the camera which usually appears on such an occasion. 'No,' called one of the little boys. 'It's over there, on the cupboard door.'

I turned. What could it be? The Sacred Heart, St Patrick, John F. Kennedy or Mother Teresa? But no. There as bold as brass and pinned to the cupboard door was a colour picture of the current team of the Liverpool Football Club.

'Oh do sign it,' said 'Super-Nan', who had recovered almost miraculously, 'I'd be right made up.'

Life is full of surprises in Liverpool, but think of the surprise that goalkeeper will have if he ever sees that photograph of himself, with the Archbishop's autograph just above his head.

Lord Jesus,
was your family life
with Joseph and your mother, Mary,
a powerful and formative human
*   experience?*
When you went down with them to Nazareth
and 'increased in wisdom and in stature
and in favour with God and men',
did they have to teach you
all those lessons about growing up
that loving parents give their sons today?
As a growing lad,
did you know the care and counsel
of your grandmother, St Anne?

What were the other childhood games
you played with boys of your own age
as you grew up in Nazareth?

By the Incarnation
and by your coming amongst us,
you brought sanctification
to family life.
Despite the inadequacy of our
    understanding,
and the pressures of contemporary
    society,
help us to regain
some of the lost strength
of our nation's family life.
Lord, what would today's statisticians
have made of your family circle
as a social unit?
A one-parent family,
father unknown?
To what social benefits
was St Joseph entitled,
and later his widow,
your mother, Mary,
to whose generous care
you entrusted us?

(Pardon our inquisitiveness, Lord,
but it is so difficult
for us to envisage
the marvel of your humanity.)

And did your extended family
meet together from time to time?
With your cousin, John the Baptist,
and the other cousins
with whom your mother lived,
when you left home
to be about your Father's business?

What did your mother think
of your choice of friends?
Did you bring Simon and Andrew,
James and John,
home to meet her?
Was there a family celebration
when you came back
from some of your journeys
with the twelve?
What was it that brought her,
with your brethren,
to seek you out
in the crowd which seemed to follow you
almost everywhere?
Was she over-anxious?
Did she really understand
those words you spoke to her
at the wedding at Cana?

So many questions, Lord,
but we need to understand
as well as trust in faith,
if we are to appreciate

the example of your human family life
and the marvel of the Incarnation.

Bless our old folk
and heads of families:
give them the support
of succeeding generations.
May the example of their dedication
help to reclaim
errant sons and daughters,
and give stability
to the wayward, the weak,
and those too easily persuaded
that it's all quite different now.

Lord, you know how difficult it can be
to respond to the overwhelming sorrow
of the bereaved.
Give us the grace to recognise
how to sustain
without taking over;
how to share the mourners' sorrow
without adding to distress;
how to give support
without being a burden;
how to show compassion
without being patronising;
how to be sympathetic and understanding
without pretence;
how to 'be there'
without intrusion.

IX

The Price
of Compassion

'When Kevin died on Christmas Eve,' said the young mum in the Bereavement Centre, 'I thought it was the end of the world.'

I was visiting a group of parents, all of whom had lost a young child in the course of the previous 18 months. They had been gathered together by a social worker in a redundant building of uncertain age attached to a children's hospital.

In such a place infant mortality can still be almost a daily feature. Even cot deaths at home are usually brought there for examination in the mortuary.

These young parents were anxious to seek my help in raising funds to equip and brighten up this rather sombre ancient building as a Centre where the parents, who would suffer the same shock and trauma as they themselves had known, might receive help and counselling.

Often, they told me, the greatest comfort which newly-bereaved parents can receive, is the experience and understanding of others who have come through the same ordeal.

There was neither melodrama nor tendency to wallow in past sorrow amongst those making up the group I had been asked to meet. The most vocal was a young father, deputed to be spokesman, whose wife held on tightly to his arm whilst he made the case for improved facilities. Quickly she took over from him when his recalling some personal recollection seemed likely to prove too much.

Another young mother, quite evidently pregnant once more and with two other small children at her side, came forward to ask me if I remembered her from her Confirmation, some ten or more years before. I could not pretend that I recognised her, though I felt flattered that she was confident that she recognised me. But she had a story to tell, and other would-be informants held back.

'When Kevin died on Christmas Eve,' she repeated, 'it was so terrible that I thought it was the end of the world. I couldn't believe that such a thing had ever happened to any other mother before.' She paused with the memory before adding, 'but the biggest surprise was when I realised how upset Father Tom was.'

I thought hastily about just which Father Tom this might be. There are quite a number, and surnames are disappearing amongst priests, as in most circles where ease of access and informality are encouraged.

'I suppose that it was because Kevin was his first,' she suggested. First what? I asked myself. Oh, the first baby he had ever baptised. That narrowed the field considerably. I tried to explain that a priest never really gets used to baptisms. Each baptism, like each funeral, is special, and brings great joy or sorrow.

'Father Tom stayed with us for most of Christmas Day,' the young mum went on. 'But when Kevin got cremated on New Year's Eve' – I could scarcely believe my ears – 'Father Tom came and did it, after we'd had Mass in the church, and he was shattered.'

By now I had this Father Tom identified and was trying to remember how many months he must have been ordained by the time all this had happened. 'I never realised,' she went on, 'that a priest cared as much as that.' 'How did it show?' I asked, somewhat anxiously, wondering if the young man had broken down and might himself still need a little help.

'Oh, it was great,' she replied, apparently almost happy with the recollection. 'That night, when it was all over, he came round to our house to see that we were all right. And he just sat on the floor and played with the other two children.' She looked fondly and proudly at the two young survivors at her side.

'It was great,' she repeated. 'It meant so much. You see, it was as if Father Tom sort of shared our sorrow with us.'

I thanked her for explaining so well how she had felt, and I readily agreed to try to help this group of parents to raise the money they needed to improve the facilities in the Bereavement Centre. There was to be no grant from central funds. 'It's easier to raise nearly one million for a highly technical computer and scanner,' one of the other parents told me, 'than to get the odd thousand we need to cheer up this old building.'

As I came away, I was thinking of an address I had been asked to give a few weeks later to a national conference of professional social workers. A government minister was billed to speak on 'The cost of the National Health Service'. I would talk on 'The price of compassion'. The Prime Minister of the day had once said that the word was patronising, but it seemed to me that to 'sort of share our suffering' described 'compassion' perfectly.

As such it was not patronising. It was priceless.

Dear Lord, all-loving Father,
You know how hard I find it
to understand,
and help others to understand,
why you sometimes call small babies to yourself,
before their parents have had a chance
to set them on their feet.
Help those sorrowing mums and dads
to accept in faith
the extent of your everlasting love
for innocence.
Comfort them in the sorrow
and the shock of their loss,

113

and give them courage
to persevere in their family life.
Lord, you know how difficult it can be
to respond to the overwhelming sorrow
of the bereaved.
Give us the grace to recognise
how to sustain
without taking over;
how to share the mourners' sorrow
without adding to distress;
how to give support
without being a burden;
how to show compassion
without being patronising;
how to be sympathetic and understanding
without pretence;
how to "be there"
without intrusion.

O Lord Jesus Christ,
High Priest of the eternal Kingdom,
guide us in the pastoral training
we give to candidates for the priesthood.
For they must surely be at all times –
in times of emergency,
just as in solemn worship –
signs of your compassion
for your people in need.

Help them to face the challenge
of being 'alter Christus',

in moments of great suffering
and of shattering perplexity:
to be schooled in the way of the Cross
so that they may know how
to reach out to those who stumble.
With their heads held high
in thoughtful concern for those about them,
and with their feet firmly planted on the ground
that others may lean upon their stability,
let them follow the path
trodden by the good Samaritan.

They need your strength
if they are to point your way.

And, Lord Jesus,
just as little children
played happily at your knee,
let those who minister in your name
know how to enable
small children and young people
to feel at home
and to be at one with them.

Lord Jesus Christ,
Give comfort to those
who still agonise
at what happened at Hillsborough.

You had no problem
in communication, Lord.
You knew all the local language and culture
of the people of Galilee.
So please help us to understand
your teaching, your love and your compassion
in the ordinary circumstances
of our daily life.
Then we shall the more readily recognise you
in the needs of those
who seek our help
and in the help of those
who respond to our needs.

X
Hillsborough

It was some years before the football ground disaster at Hillsborough that a young priest suggested to me that there was an interesting and significant parallel between a local 'Derby' match, involving the Liverpool and Everton Football clubs, and a celebration of the liturgy.

He explained. The congregation gathers in a mixture of excitement and awe. The master of ceremonies, rather like the referee, comes out to examine the sanctuary – or was it the pitch? The Kop end at Anfield strikes up the entrance hymn. The response is entrusted to the visiting supporters at the other end of the ground. The ministers (or players) enter as the rite begins.

'You can work it all out for yourself,' said the young priest, whose liturgical colour, as a Liverpool supporter, was red. 'With one or two exceptions,' he added, 'there's a parallel right the way through; and if it's a benefit match, there's even a retiring collection before you leave the ground.'

I allowed my thoughts to drift towards the homily which presumably was delivered to the players by their manager in the dressing room at half-time. I even found myself wondering about the formula to be used when the sign of peace was to be exchanged at the end...

That was several years ago now. But I remembered the conversation when, some days after the Hillsborough disaster, the Government sent a judge to enquire into the circumstances in which so many young enthusiasts had lost their lives.

For when I was invited to Anfield to meet him, the learned visitor challenged me, 'Archbishop, aren't you jealous of football as a rival religion?'

Mercifully I did not have to answer. Whilst I was thinking of comparative examples, favourable and unfavourable, with which to repel this verbal assault, the Chairman of the Football Club came to my rescue. He had apparently overheard what was presumably intended merely as a passing pleasantry, and swept the challenge to one side.

'No, Judge,' he replied for me, with remarkable assurance, 'you have got it all wrong. In this city football and religion are both accepted as part of our normal daily life. So the question of rivalry just doesn't arise.' With which he swept the judge into lunch with the same sureness of touch as he had just employed to rule the suspected assault offside.

Meantime I had consoling thoughts about the integration of religious faith in the life of many of our people, who are nevertheless often uncertain in the expression of their belief, and sometimes even filled with self-doubt about their having absorbed the faith of their fathers.

Later that same afternoon I was telephoned by the city's emergency counselling service, which had been set up to deal with those apparently suffering from what was popularly being called 'trauma'. These were persons who had been present when the disaster occurred and who were suffering from shock and sometimes guilt at being part of the crowd, pushing to get into the ground and contributing to the fatal crush experienced by those trapped against the barriers in front of them.

The counselling service was anxious that I should try to help a young man who had seen the whole disaster at Hillsborough, the previous Saturday afternoon, take place before him. One of his close friends had been killed. He was still suffering from shock and also from shame at having himself survived the tragedy.

When the crowd had at last dispersed on that terrible afternoon, he had just sat down outside the ground and wept. How was he to tell his friend's family what he had seen? Eventually someone had given him a lift back home, but by the time he arrived, he was unable to speak. His wife had sat him down in front of his television set in the hope of reawakening some response in him.

It seems that he was still sitting there bemused the next evening when Mass from Liverpool's Metropolitan Cathedral came on the screen. He claimed that my words on that occasion had brought him out of his semi-coma. Subsequently the counselling service, to which he had been directed by his wife, sent him round to see me so that he might talk a little more.

'It was something you said that night,' he explained to me. 'I think I've got the words right. They seemed suddenly to break through from your world to mine.'

I might as well admit now that I was at once keen to know what spiritual insights I had achieved. 'It was when you spoke about your visit to the hospital in Sheffield, where the casualties had been taken,' he said, 'and you talked about how the nurses were getting used to the ways of their young Scouse patients.' 'Yes, I remember,' I encouraged him. 'Well,' he continued, 'it was when you said that the nurses, as they handed out cups of tea, heard the Liverpool lads say, "Thanks, luv, for the bevvy".'

Then he added with great simplicity, 'It was your using our word. That's what brought me out of my nightmare and confusion. I could recognise what you meant. It stirred something inside of me and it made sense.'

Life can be complex these days. It is when faith becomes articulate and coherent, that religion, like football, is recognisable as part of our life. So whilst I thought about Incarnation and local culture, we talked about Liverpool words, and about how half the pitch at Anfield was covered with flowers.

'Rather like a Corpus Christi procession,' I suggested. And he did not ask me to explain.

Lord Jesus Christ,
by your Incarnation
you came to share our life:
you must have felt the pressure
of the great crowds who thronged about you.
Give comfort to those
who still agonise
at what happened at Hillsborough.

You had no problem
in communication, Lord.
You knew all the local language and culture
of the people of Galilee.
So please help us to understand
your teaching, your love and your compassion
in the ordinary circumstances
of our daily life.
Then we shall the more readily recognise you
in the needs of those
who seek our help,
and in the help of those
who respond to our needs.

We know that when a gap opens
between your teaching and our worship,
between your truths and our daily life,
it is because we have turned our backs on you.
Sometimes we do not do that
intentionally or even consciously.
We let ourselves become
so taken up with all the good things

with which you have filled our lives,
that what starts as a distraction
or leisure time interest,
can so fill our vision
as to blind us to the donor.
Help us to remember, O Lord,
so that we may keep our heads,
our balance
and a true sense of proportion.

When we lose sight of our landmarks, Lord,
which we have put down from precious
*   experience,*
give us courage
to look more closely at you
and to persevere in faith

until we find them
showing up the path we must follow.

When we lose our loved ones, Lord,
grant that we may remember
that they are safe with you:
safer, better cared for, and more dearly loved
than we can ever achieve
on our own.

You came to share our life, Lord,
our sorrows and our joys.
Let us never shut you out,
especially when you seek to use us
as instruments
of your mercy and your love.

For you, above all,
know the way to the hearts
of your wayward people.

This is the gift of perseverance, Lord,
which your priests need
in face of the instability of others.
Help us all to understand
that an occasional coming together in worship
is not enough:
that it is our need of you
and not your need of us
which must bring us to our knees.
For where true love is in possession,
there are no off duty moments,
no dispensations from our required response
of obedience and devotion.

XI
Solidarity

'You're looking very tired,' I said to the leader of a group of priests responsible for a thickly populated area of the inner city. 'Having too many late nights?' I asked, knowing him well enough to be confident that such light-hearted chiding was enough to indicate that I understood the heavy demands made of him.

'You can say that again,' he countered with a weary grin. 'At the beginning of the week we were up till the small hours three nights running.'

This puzzled me slightly, since I knew that there was no hospital in the parish, nor in his deanery for that matter. He moved quickly to reassure me. 'We were up all hours hearing confessions before Millie's funeral.'

I must have looked mystified, for he went on, 'You remember Millie, don't you?' I tried to look mindful, without much success. 'She was the one we used to call the Queen of Scotland Road,' he explained. 'She ran the pub. She had done so for years. In many ways she had become a sort of Coronation Street Annie Walker for our area. Millie knew everyone and everyone knew her. It wasn't that she was particularly nosy or anything like that. It was just that "The Clarrie" – the "Duke of Clarence", you understand – was one of the best known meeting-places in the whole district.'

He thought for a bit. Then he continued, 'Millie had been there so long that she knew all about everyone and everything, past and present; and she gave the impression of having a pretty good idea about what was being hatched up for the future as well.'

'Was she one of us?' I asked, perhaps unnecessarily.

'Oh yes,' he replied thoughtfully, 'though I must admit that there were some quite long times when it wasn't very noticeable. She claimed that she didn't find the "changes" helpful, though I doubt if they would have made much difference to her. For instance, she didn't know a word of Latin, but she had come to think of it as the language which her particular tribe used in Church. And I'm afraid that she wasn't too sure about your brand of ecumenism. She was of "green" stock, and to Millie the others were "orange" and Protestant.'

Millie's uneasiness was largely due to the fact that most of the local employers were either from the Protestant establishment or, in her eyes still worse, from the south of England. Every time she heard that her Church was becoming slightly more middle class, she became increasingly vehement about the so-called 'Mersey miracle'. 'Not that it made much difference to her church-going,' he added. 'She had belonged to the "special occasion" group of Catholics for a long time.'

'You mean christenings and weddings,' I said.
'Something like that,' he replied, 'and of course funerals.'

The priest went on to explain that it was not just for the death of family and friends that our

Millie had felt it right to give public witness to her faith. There were certain almost tribal occasions when everyone who was anyone in the area felt under obligation to be there and in some manner involved. Even if you were 'one of them', he explained, it was the done thing to be out on the pavement when the hearse and attendant limousines made their slow mournful way to the Church.

'Millie's funeral yesterday was like that.' He thought for a moment and then added as his evaluation of the importance of the occasion, 'There were seventeen car-loads of mourners and an extra two hearses for the flowers.'

'That's a lot,' I agreed. 'I suppose all the crowds were out to see the procession go by.'

'Yes,' he replied, 'Millie came home to us in great style, worthy of the best traditions of the area.'

I asked whether he had managed to pack them all into his church, but he told me quickly that that was not the problem. For reason of age or infirmity, or just because so many of them had become 'occasionals' rather than 'regulars', great numbers of people had wanted to go to confession before the funeral Mass.

This was where the priest had shown his deep knowledge and understanding of his people. 'You have to try to get some of the confessions over before the morning of the funeral or else the Mass gets delayed,' he explained. 'So our custom is to go round to the house where the wake is being held. Sometimes you need to do that for several evenings before the funeral.'

I began to understand why this priest looked so tired and what he had meant when he had claimed to have been up for three nights running at the beginning of the week.

'Yes,' he admitted, 'they gave us a couple of rooms upstairs over the pub, and the pair of us were at it, hearing confessions, till the small hours.' He paused before saying somewhat tentatively, 'I suppose that was all right, wasn't it? It's what we often have to do before a big funeral.'

I thanked God silently for a couple of priests who knew and understood their people so well, and asked him if it all worked out satisfactorily in the end.

'Well, we dealt with most of the family and close friends upstairs beforehand. But still more turned up at the church in the morning, just ahead of the hearse. They wanted confession too, so that they could go to communion at what had become the funeral of the year.' Then he explained, 'The difficulty always is to judge when to stop hearing confessions in order to get the Mass started.'

I decided not to ask the obvious question about general absolution, and simply said, 'I'm sure that you had it all worked out satisfactorily.'

He grinned at the unspoken reassurance and said that everyone seemed well satisfied. They would be all right now – at least until the next tribal occasion brought them all back again. 'Solidarity,' he said.

It would be easy to discount Millie's funeral as an example of urban tribalism, and the diagnosis would be wrong. As I watched the priest return to Scottie Road, as he called it, my mind dwelt on the meaning of that word 'solidarity'. Though often identified with the worker movement which began in the dockyard of Gdańsk in Poland, it describes very well the relationship between those who have learned to stand together in face of threat or adversity.

The episode was still fresh in my mind when, some months later, Mrs Margaret Thatcher poured scorn on the work force in the Liverpool docks for having joined a national dock strike over an issue of no direct local concern. She described it as being typical of the militancy of the whole area.

It so happened that I had the opportunity soon afterwards to challenge her about this. I pointed out that often what appeared to others to be industrial militancy was merely an expression of worker solidarity, bred of decades of hardship.

Not surprisingly, she seemed unimpressed and replied sharply, 'If that is what you call "solidarity", then the word is nothing more than an antiquated shibboleth.' She did however accept my advice not to employ that colourful phrase in a further address to be delivered in the area later that same day.

She will not have known that I had in mind the crowds who had come out in their hundreds as the undertaker's hearse went by, to express their solidarity with Millie as, Queen of Scotland Road, she finally came home.

Or was I really thinking of the upper room of 'The Clarrie' during the wake, and the efforts of the two priests to hold their people together in what really mattered?

Lord Jesus Christ,
high priest of the new and eternal covenant,
with wisdom and love
you have planned
that this one priesthood
should continue in the Church.

You have chosen humble men
to share your sacred ministry,
and to lead your holy people in love
and to feed them with your word.

No one can be worthy of such a calling,
nor be personally adequate
to share in this greatest of all gifts.
But if we are to share
in this sign of your confidence
*   and trust in us,*
grant us also a share in your compassion
and of the love and understanding
you showed to the needy and distressed.

Strengthen and sustain us, Lord,
as we reach out with words of
*   encouragement*
to those who have turned away from you.
Give us patience and courage
when our forbearance and restraint
earns for us from others
the contemptuous mockery
of being a 'wet' or a weak-kneed 'wimp'.

Dear Lord, you cast no stone
at the woman taken in adultery.
You rewarded with renewed responsibility
the penitent Simon Peter,
whose impetuosity and faith
had failed him in the moment of challenge.
Forgive us our infidelities and shortcomings
as we forgive those
who are unfaithful to us,
or who fall short
of the standards we uphold in your name.

Help us to sustain the disappointments
and punishments meted out to us
because of your teaching.

Grant us the willingness to come back for more:
to persevere in our practice of the sacraments,
and never to be harsh and condemnatory
with those who presume on your mercy,
or who take for granted
the generosity of your forgiveness.

This is the gift of perseverance, Lord,
which your priests need
in face of the instability of others.
Help us all to understand
that an occasional coming together in worship
is not enough:
that it is our need of you
and not your need of us
which must bring us to our knees.
For where true love is in possession,
there are no off duty moments,
no dispensations from our required response
of obedience and devotion.

So, on our knees now, dear Lord,
we ask for ourselves a constant realisation
that you understand and care about
    the times
when we let ourselves become too busy
to follow faithfully
your pilgrim way.
You took to yourself
our human flesh
and know well our weaknesses.

Your incarnation is the greatest expression
of the solidarity of humankind.
Give us grateful faithful hearts:
for our debt is overwhelming.

Before all else, Lord,
help me to recognise
the presence of your guiding hand
in my normal daily round
and in what I take for granted.
Let me not be looking for thanks,
content just to be
an instrument of your justice and your love.
But when, by your mercy,
praise and thanks are forthcoming,
help me to know how to receive
as well as to give, generously.

And make sure that I appreciate
that it is due to your love, Lord,
when, for the goodness of your people,
I'm 'made up'.

XII

Bread cast
upon the Waters

'**H**ullo,' said my escort, with a question in his voice, 'trouble?'

I looked ahead to where a small police car was drawn up outside the row of shops where we were due to pull in. Over a newsagent, just where the police car was parked, was the office of the group of social workers who had asked for a visit that afternoon.

I could think of no obvious reason why these servants of the community should attract the attention of the custodians of the law; though I recalled an earlier occasion elsewhere, when my visit to a hostel for ex-prisoners coincided with the re-arrest of a number of them, for questioning in connection with a recent alleged offence.

That earlier occasion had, as I remembered, called for tact, understanding and a certain sense of humour. These qualities had all been needed to ease the obvious embarrassment of the organisers. I had learned afterwards that one of their other 'guests', overlooked by the police, had been so impressed by my cheerfulness that the following day he had wagered all his precious discharge grant on a horse called 'Benign Bishop'. This had had disastrous consequences to his faith, as the animal had fallen at the first fence.

But this time our anxiety was without foundation. After a quick encounter with some trainee photographers at the entrance, we went quickly upstairs to the office above. There we met officers of the organisation which had invited me to take an interest in its work of re-settling 'roofless' youngsters, who had abandoned or been thrown out of their homes.

A quick look round the room revealed not only the Mayor, with chain of office and all, but also tucked away in the corner of the room a uniformed policeman, with his cap tucked under his arm as a sign of peaceful intent.

This explained the vehicle outside.

'If only central government would give us a proper grant,' began the officials of the organisation, 'we could increase the provision, and thereby save some of the youngsters from going down to London in the belief that they will get a new start in life, and enjoy the hoped-for freedom which comes from anonymity in a large city.'

'How do you place them here?' I asked; and these patient but enthusiastic men and women explained the whole process, beginning with their finding the sort of person who used to be called 'a good landlady'. This was of course someone who was prepared to take a roofless lad into her home, treat him as a member of the family until the organisation could get him a job. Then in due time they would fix him up in a room or flat of his own.

'Do you manage to find many such fairy god-mothers nowadays?' I asked, and thereby un-leashed a feast of telling statistics, drawn from the previous five years. These would prove uncommonly useful next time I might encounter the

Minister for Housing, or had to make a broadcast appeal for Homes for the Homeless.

'Wait a minute. It is always more effective to put a little flesh on figures,' said my informant, colouring slightly at the possibility of a double meaning.

He need not have worried. He beckoned to a young woman across the room and introduced her to me as someone who, having seen two young men successfully launched on their own, after spending three or four months in her family, had called into the office that afternoon to say that she and her husband were willing to take on another.

My eyes wandered towards the young policeman who seemed to be following the conversation closely. He stood patiently to one side, periodically nodding as if in support of the case which was being represented to me.

Time was strictly limited and seemed to be running out. More visits to community projects were planned for me. A young man had just been brought in by one of his mates, in the hope that he might be persuaded to accept help and give up the independence of 'roofless' people. There was an amount of healing to be done.

I thanked my informants and congratulated them on what had been achieved so far. I promised to do my best to make known their record in areas where help might be forthcoming. Did they believe, I asked, that the proposed abolition of

the Poll Tax would in time have the effect that fewer youngsters would be put out of their own homes by troubled parents? Probably, but there was still quite widespread drug abuse in the region.

As I was leaving, I turned and went across to the policeman whose presence had caused my companion some anxiety initially and who was still being regarded with suspicion by the young man who had just been brought in.

'Thank you very much for coming in here this afternoon,' I began. Then, laughing, I asked him, 'Did you think perhaps that my safety might be threatened, or that I might cause a breach of the peace?'

He continued to finger his somewhat nervous

way around the brim of the cap in his hand. 'No, Father,' he said, 'but I just knew that I couldn't face my mother if I didn't come in to see you. You see, when we got word of your visit, she told me to make sure that I didn't miss you and to give you her love.'

Slightly taken aback, I thanked him and he came to my rescue. 'Mrs Wood,' he explained, and I tried to look knowledgeable. 'I think she nursed you in hospital some years ago.' By now I remembered the name only vaguely, but I was able to establish which hospital, and that it was about ten years earlier. In return I sent suitable greetings to his mother and he told me that by now she was retired. Gradually the story began to come together. His mother had asked him to remind me of the letter which I had written to her some weeks afterwards. But which letter? I wondered: twenty or thirty a day was the average.

Suddenly it all came back to me. 'Was the letter about you?' I asked, and for the first time he smiled confidently and nodded. 'But you weren't in the police then,' I added, trying hard to clear my memory.

'No,' he replied, 'I was training as a nurse, and there was trouble over my marriage. My wife had left me. I was trying to look after our child and working for my nursing exams at the same time...' He broke off as someone edged close to my elbow to say that it was time for me to move on.

'How are things now?' I asked him.

'Fine,' he replied, 'all sorted out. We followed the advice in your letter. As you can see, I joined the police instead. So Mum suggested that I should come in today to say "Thank you" and to see how you are.'

'I'm fine too,' I told him. 'Tell your mother that I remember and that I am so glad that things have worked out.' I shook his hand and he followed me downstairs, his mission completed. 'She'll be made up when I tell her,' he said, and encouraged by the remembrance, I moved on to the next port of call for that afternoon, a number of training projects run by the local authority.

Each of the schemes had its interest and value. There were questions to be asked, encouragement to be given, greetings to be exchanged, even combined ecumenical anti-litter activities to be carried out with the local binmen for the benefit of the attendant photographers. With a splendid pair of municipal tongs, we collected rubbish and picked up discarded bread-crusts floating in an outsize puddle on a piece of wasteland.

It was late in the afternoon when at last we were taken into a youth centre, where a group of youngsters told us of their leisure activities, ranging from fell walking by the Lakes to ballet dancing and mime. I sat down for a rest and watched in fascination as these young people performed for our entertainment with great grace and energy. They were due to give a further display that evening and had been trained skilfully by a young teacher who danced with them that afternoon.

At last they concluded and took their well-earned applause, and I moved forward to have a word with some of them as they recovered their breath. I was suddenly aware that my escort was again at my shoulder. 'There's a young lady here who would like a word with you,' he said.

The young teacher approached and we drew to one side. Her eyes filled as she said, 'Oh, I'm so sorry, I am filled with emotion.' Then after a pause she added, 'I just wanted to say "Thank you".' And she put her arms round my neck and kissed me.

'On the contrary,' I replied, as gallantly as possible, 'I should thank you for the dancing. It was beautiful.' I was aware that several pairs of eyes were riveted upon us.

'I have waited several years for this chance to thank you,' she went on, and I realised that more was at stake than I had assumed. 'Do you remember me?' she asked and, seeing my puzzled look, came quickly to my help. 'No, of course you couldn't be expected to.' She paused. 'You helped me through college. It was just after my Dad died and I couldn't have gone on with my training. But you made it possible. I'm so grateful.'

The tears came again as she told me of her struggle to finish her studies after her father's death, and how, when she had qualified, she had been employed by the local authority as a teacher. Now she had been given the opportunity to help these youngsters by training them in dance and mime.

And I began to recall how at a parish visitation, one of the priests had told me of a parishioner's unexpected death and how the daughter would need financial help if she was to complete her studies. Mercifully, at that time some money had been given me for use at my discretion. I had been taught by my first bishop that such monies should not be allowed to gather dust or rust. Now the fruit of this benefaction stood before me…

'What was that all about?' one of my companions asked me afterwards. I knew that I could not really begin to explain how I felt. Twice in an afternoon. It could not easily be explained.

'Just cast your bread upon the waters,' I said rather mysteriously. I suspect he began to think of the binmen and those wretched crusts floating in the puddle on the waste land.

As for me, this time it was I who was 'made up'.

Dear God our Father,
give me a grateful heart:
filled with thanks
for all the support with which you surround me,
and for all the people
anxious to share with me
their experience of responsibility,
the fruits of their service
to the disadvantaged and needy.
Help me to be an encouragement to them.
Grant that I may shed upon their problems
the light of your Son's gospel.

Especially when the hardship of others
weighs heavily upon me,
grant that I may be for them
a sign of hope,
so that I may know how best
to encourage their perseverance.
To each new initiative,
undertaken for sake of the community,
keep my vision open wide.
Grant that I may be a good listener,
humble enough to still my own pressing desires,
ready to learn from others,
helpful with positive suggestions,
sparing with criticism,
not damning with faint praise.

Help me to convey your joy and your concern
to every worthwhile project,

regardless of who has thought it out.
Stir up my enthusiasm
for what is intended to give service to the
  community –
even though I have seen it all before –
several times, Lord.

Remind me constantly
that behind all the planning
with which I am assailed,
real people are involved:
human beings created by you,
with individual and immortal souls
whether they know it or not.

Let me be careful and caring
with counsel and concern,
generous with resources at my disposal
and mindful that it is you
who have placed them in my charge.

Help me to be patient and understanding
when my expectations of others
have not been fulfilled.
Let me be as generous in my response
to unrelenting calls for assistance,
as I expect to find in the commitment of others
in my own regard.
Let my response be prompt, Lord,
especially when the needs of others
do not fit my timetable,
nor meet my convenience.

Before all else, Lord,
help me to recognise
the presence of your guiding hand
in my normal daily round
and in what I take for granted.
Let me not be looking for thanks,
content just to be
an instrument of your justice and your love.
But when, by your mercy,
praise and thanks are forthcoming,
help me to know how to receive
as well as to give, generously.

And make sure that I appreciate
that it is due to your love, Lord,
when, for the goodness of your people,
I'm 'made up'.